Blending Colors Hat,
page 21

Spiraling
Cowl,
page 16

Peaked
Waves
Slippers,
page 30

Learn to
TAPESTRY
CROCHET

Table of Contents

Tapestry Crochet Basics

Tapestry crochet is a wonderful technique that will allow you to add colorwork to your projects. One or more strands of yarn are carried and wrapped in the stitches of the working color. Then, colors are switched by following a pattern to make a specific design. There are no floats on the wrong side of the work, and you make a stronger weave.

Depending on the piece you are making, you will crochet one or more foundation rows or rounds without carrying any alternate color and then move on to the tapestry portion of the project.

There are several ways to work with this technique, and in this book we will cover 3 variations:

- Tapestry crochet with single crochet worked in rows

- Tapestry crochet with back loop single crochet worked in the round

- Tapestry crochet with back loop double crochet worked in the round

Basic Steps to Carry & Wrap the Additional Yarn

Tapestry crochet with single crochet worked in rows

After the foundation row, start the first row of the tapestry pattern. Chain 1 and start the first single crochet: Insert the hook in the stitch, yarn over and pull through the stitch *(see photo 1)*,

Photo 1

leaving a 4-inch tail, place the new color in between your hook and the working yarn *(see photo 2)*,

Photo 2

yarn over with the working yarn and close the first single crochet *(see photos 3 and 4)*.

Photo 3

Photo 4

Your alternate color is now wrapped in the first single crochet.

To continue, insert your hook in the next stitch, working under the alternate color *(see photo 5)*, and complete the single crochet with the strand wrapped again *(see photo 6)*. Repeat for each single crochet across.

Photo 5

Photo 6

Tapestry crochet with back loop single crochet worked in the round

After the foundation round or rounds, start the first round of the tapestry pattern. Begin the first single crochet as follows: Chain 1, insert the hook in the back loop of the same stitch as the join, yarn over and pull up a loop (see photo 7),

Photo 7

leaving a 4-inch tail, place the new color between your hook and the working yarn (see photo 8),

Photo 8

yarn over with the working yarn (see photo 9) and close the first back loop single crochet (see photo 10). Your alternate color is now wrapped in the first back loop single crochet.

Photo 9

Photo 10

Place a marker in the first back loop single crochet of each round, as it will be useful when closing rounds.

To continue, insert your hook in the back loop of next single crochet, working under the alternate color *(see photo 11)*, and complete the back loop single crochet with the strand wrapped again *(see photo 12)*. Repeat for each single crochet across.

Photo 11

Photo 12

Tapestry crochet with back loop double crochet worked in the round

After the foundation round, start the first round of the tapestry pattern. Chain 3 and start a double crochet in the back loop of the next stitch: Yarn over, insert the hook in the back loop, yarn over and pull through the stitch *(see photo 13)*,

Photo 13

leaving a 4-inch tail, place the new color in between your hook and the working yarn *(see photo 14)*,

Photo 14

yarn over with the working yarn *(see photo 15)* and pull through two loops on the hook, yarn over and pull through the last two loops on the hook *(see photo 16)*. Your alternate color is now wrapped in the back loop double crochet.

Photo 15

Photo 16

To continue, yarn over and insert your hook in the back loop of next stitch, working under the alternate color *(see photo 17)*, and complete the back loop double crochet with the strand wrapped again *(see photo 18)*. Repeat for each stitch across.

Photo 17

Photo 18

Color Changes

Do the same in every variation: Work the last stitch before the color change to just before the last yarn over, drop the working color, yarn over with the new color *(see photo 19)* and close the stitch *(see photo 20)*. Then wrap the other color instead and switch colors again according to the pattern *(see photos 21 and 22)*.

Photo 19

Photo 20

Photo 21

Photo 22

Tip: *Use a system that prevents yarn from getting tangled with the colorwork. Ball holders (see photo 23) keep each color in the same position for the whole project and make it easy to pick each yarn from its source to switch.*

Photo 23

Ending & Beginning of Rows & Rounds

Tapestry crochet with single crochet worked in rows

Work to the last single crochet by wrapping the alternate color *(see photo 24)*, turn.

Photo 24

Chain 1 and start the first single crochet: Insert the hook in the stitch, working under the yarn to be wrapped *(see photo 25)*,

Photo 25

yarn over with the working yarn *(see photo 26)* and complete the single crochet with the strand wrapped again *(see photo 27)*. Your alternate color is wrapped from the first single crochet of every row.

Photo 26

Photo 27

Tapestry crochet with back loop single crochet worked in the round

Work to the last single crochet of the round by wrapping the alternate color or colors *(see photo 28)*,

Photo 28

remove the marker of the first back loop single crochet, insert your hook in the stitch by working under both loops and the alternate color *(see photo 29)*, yarn over with the working yarn *(see photo 30)* and pull through the stitch, making a slip stitch to close *(see photo 31)*.

Photo 29

Photo 30

Photo 31

Now you are ready to start the next round with the alternate color in place to be wrapped in the first back loop single crochet.

Tapestry crochet with back loop double crochet worked in the round

Work to the last double crochet of the round by wrapping the alternate color *(see photo 32)*,

Photo 32

insert your hook in the 3rd beginning chain, working under the alternate color *(see photo 33)*,

Photo 33

yarn over with the working yarn *(see photo 34)* and pull through the chain making a slip stitch to close *(see photo 35)*.

Photo 34

Photo 35

Now you are ready to start the next round with the alternate color in place to be wrapped in the first back loop double crochet.

**Tapestry crochet with single crochet
worked in rows**

**Tapestry crochet with back loop single crochet
worked in the round**

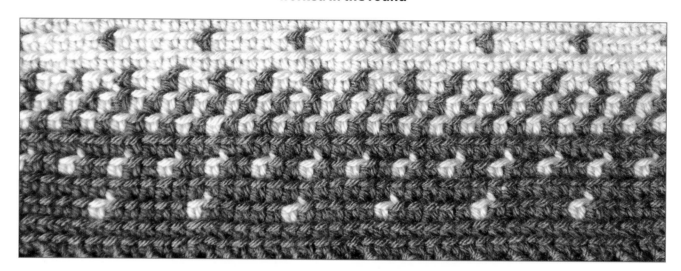

**Tapestry crochet with back loop double crochet
worked in the round**

Additional Notes

Eyelets (for Tie-Up Choker and Drawstring Bag):
Work under the alternate color or yarns with your hook, yarn over with the working yarn *(see photo 36)* and complete a single crochet with the yarn wrapped *(see photo 37)*.

Photo 38

Photo 36

Photo 39

Photo 37

Repeat for the number of single crochets indicated in the pattern *(see photo 38)* and skip the same amount of single crochets from the last row or round, then continue crocheting over the single crochet of last row or round *(see photo 39)*.

Wrapped Yarn: Depending on the yarn you're working with, you will see more or less of the underlying color or colors when working tapestry crochet with single crochet. This is normal and it's not necessary to pull the alternate color unless you see a very obvious bump. When working in double crochet, where stitches are a bit more open, pull the yarn a little after making some stitches to straighten the bumps that show through the other color in your work.

Fastening Off: When finishing the tapestry crochet portion of the project, cut the wrapped yarn(s), leaving a 4-inch tail. Weave in the ends. ●

Tie-Up Choker

Skill Level

■■■□ INTERMEDIATE

Finished Measurements

Choker: 12¼ inches wide x 1¼ inches long

Tie-Up Lace: 18½ inches long

Materials

- Omega Eulali super fine (fingering) weight cotton yarn (3½ oz/ 394 yds/100g per skein):
  1 skein each #18 cream and #94 steel
- Size C/2/2.75mm crochet hook or size needed to obtain gauge
- Tapestry needle

Gauge

31 sts = 4 inches; 7 rows = 1 inch

Pattern Notes

Foundation row and last row are worked with 1 strand of yarn without carrying alternate color.

Weave in ends as work progresses.

When changing color in Pattern Stitch, carry and work over color not in use on wrong side of tapestry crochet section. Do not cut or fasten off unless otherwise stated.

Choker Pattern can be worked by following written instructions or Chart. Follow Chart rows 1, 3, 5 and 7 from right to left and rows 2, 4 and 6 from left to right.

Pattern Stitch

Choker Pattern

Row 1: With steel, ch 1, sc in each of first 4 sc, **change color** *(see page 5 and Pattern Notes)* to cream in last st, sc in each of next 89 sc, change color to steel, sc in each of last 4 sc, turn. *(97 sc)*

Row 2 (RS): With steel, ch 1, sc in first sc, working over cream, work 2 sc *(see photos 37 and 38 on page 9—eyelet made)*, sk 2 sc, sc in each of next 4 sc, [change color to cream, sc in each of next 3 sc, change color to steel, sc in each of next 5 sc] 10 times, change color to cream, sc in each of next 3 sc, change color to steel, sc in each of next 4 sc, working over cream, work 2 sc *(eyelet made)*, sk 2 sc, sc in last sc, turn.

Row 3: With steel, ch 1, sc in each of first 4 sc, change color to cream, sc in each of next 2 sc, [change color to steel, sc in next sc, change color to cream, sc in each of next 3 sc] 21 times, change color to steel, sc in next sc, change color to cream, sc in each of next 2 sc, change color to steel, sc in each of last 4 sc, turn.

Rows 4 & 5: Rep row 3.

Row 6: With steel, ch 1, sc in first sc, working over cream, work 2 sc *(eyelet made)*, sk 2 sc, sc in next sc, change color to cream, sc in each of next 2 sc, [change color to steel, sc in each of next 5 sc, change color to cream, sc in each of next 3 sc] 10 times, change color to steel, sc in each of next 5 sc, change color to cream, sc in each of next 2 sc, change color to steel, sc in next sc, working over cream, work 2 sc *(eyelet made)*, sk 2 sc, sc in last sc, turn.

Row 7: Rep row 1.

Choker

With steel, ch 98.

Foundation row (RS): Starting in 2nd ch from hook, sc in each ch across, turn. *(97 sc)*

Rows 1–7: Work rows 1–7 of **Choker Pattern** *(see Pattern Stitch)*. Cut cream at end of row 7.

Last row: With steel, ch 1, sc in each sc across. Fasten off.

Tie-Up Lace

With cream, ch 161.

Row 1: Starting in 2nd ch from hook, sl st in each ch across. Fasten off. *(160 sl sts)*

Assembly

On RS of Choker, pull each end of Tie-Up Lace through each lower eyelet (front to back). Cross the lace once, pull each end through each upper eyelet (front to back) and tie. ●

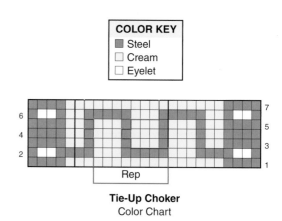

COLOR KEY
- ■ Steel
- ☐ Cream
- ☐ Eyelet

Tie-Up Choker
Color Chart

Diamond Bracelet

Skill Level

 INTERMEDIATE

Finished Measurements

2¾ inches wide x 7½ inches long, unsnapped

Materials

- Omega Eulali super fine (fingering) weight cotton yarn (3½ oz/ 394 yds/100g per skein): 1 skein each #21 sand and #55 grape
- Sizes C/2/2.75mm and H/8/5mm crochet hooks or size needed to obtain gauge
- Tapestry needle
- 10mm snaps: 2 sets
- Sewing needle and matching thread

Gauge

Size C hook: 31 sts = 4 inches; 7 rows = 1 inch

Pattern Notes

Foundation row and last row are worked with 1 strand of yarn without carrying alternate color.

Weave in ends as work progresses.

When changing color in Pattern Stitch, carry and work over color not in use on wrong side of tapestry crochet section. Do not cut or fasten off unless otherwise stated.

Diamond Pattern can be worked by following written instructions or Chart. Follow Chart rows 1, 3, 5, 7, 9, 11 and 13 from right to left and rows 2, 4, 6, 8, 10 and 12 from left to right.

Pattern Stitch

Diamond Pattern

Row 1: With grape, ch 1, sc in each of first 5 sc, [**change color** *(see page 5 and Pattern Notes)* to sand in last st, sc in next sc, change color to grape, sc in each of next 2 sc, change color to sand, sc in each of next 2 sc, change color to grape, sc in each of next 2 sc, change color to sand, sc in each of next 3 sc, change color to grape, sc in each of next 2 sc, change color to sand, sc in each of next 2 sc, change color to grape, sc in each of next 2 sc] 3 times, change color to sand, sc in next sc, change color to grape, sc in each of last 5 sc, turn. *(59 sc)*

Row 2 (RS): With grape, ch 1, sc in each of first 7 sc, [change color to sand, sc in each of next 2 sc, change color to grape, sc in each of next 2 sc, change color to sand, sc in each of next 2 sc, change color to grape, sc in next sc, change color to sand, sc in each of next 2 sc, change color to grape, sc in each of next 2 sc, change color to sand, sc in each of next 2 sc, change color to grape, sc in each of next 3 sc] twice, change color to sand, sc in each of next 2 sc, change color to grape, sc in each of next 2 sc, change color to sand, sc in each of next 2 sc, change color to grape, sc in next sc, change color to sand, sc in each of next 2 sc, change color to grape, sc in each of next 2 sc, change color to sand, sc in each of next 2 sc, change color to grape, sc in each of last 7 sc, turn.

Row 3: With grape, ch 1, sc in each of first 6 sc, [change color to sand, sc in each of next 2 sc, change color to grape, sc in each of next 2 sc, change color to sand, sc in each of next 2 sc, change color to grape, sc in each of next 3 sc, change color to sand, sc in each of next 2 sc, change color to grape, sc in each of next 2 sc, change color to sand, sc in each of next 2 sc, change color to grape, sc in next sc] twice, change color to sand, sc in each of next 2 sc, change color to grape, sc in each of next 2 sc, change color to sand, sc in each of next 2 sc, change color to grape, sc in each of next 3 sc, change color to sand, sc in each of next 2 sc, change color to grape, sc in each of next 2 sc, change color to sand, sc in each of next 2 sc, change color to grape, sc in each of last 6 sc, turn.

Row 4: With grape, ch 1, sc in each of first 5 sc, change color to sand, sc in each of next 2 sc, [change color to grape, sc in each of next 2 sc, change color to sand, sc in each of next 2 sc, change color to grape, sc in each of next 2 sc, change color to sand, sc in next sc, change color to grape, sc in each of next 2 sc, change color to sand, sc in each of next 2 sc, change color to grape, sc in each of next 2 sc, change color to sand, sc in each of next 3 sc] twice, change color to grape, sc in each of next 2 sc, change color to sand, sc in each of next 2 sc, change color to grape, sc in each of next 2 sc, change color to sand, sc in next sc, [change color to grape, sc in each of next 2 sc, change color to sand, sc in each of next 2 sc] twice, change color to grape, sc in each of last 5 sc, turn.

Rows 5–7: Rep rows 1–3.

Row 8: Rep row 2.

Row 9: Rep row 1.

Row 10: Rep row 4.

Row 11: Rep row 3.

Row 12: Rep row 2.

Row 13: Rep row 1.

Bracelet

With grape and C hook, ch 60.

Foundation row: Starting in 2nd ch from hook, sc in each ch across, turn. *(59 sc)*

Rows 1–13: Work rows 1–13 of **Diamond Pattern** *(see Pattern Stitch)*. Cut sand at end of row 13.

Last row: With grape, ch 1, sc in each sc across. Fasten off.

Chain Edging
Make 2.

Cut 6 39⅜-inch-long strips of sand. With strips tog and H hook, ch 26, leaving a 2⅜-inch tail at beg. Fasten off. Tie a knot on each end. Trim ends evenly.

Assembly

On RS of Bracelet, with 2 strands of grape, sew each Chain Edging to upper and lower edges of Bracelet, along width of Diamond Pattern only.

Sew snap pieces 3 rows from upper and lower edges so grape sections overlap. ●

COLOR KEY
■ Grape
□ Sand

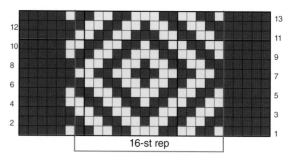

16-st rep

Diamond Bracelet
Color Chart

Spiraling Cowl

Skill Level

 INTERMEDIATE

Finished Measurements

6 inches wide x 53½ inches in circumference

Materials

- Universal Yarn Uptown Worsted medium (worsted) weight acrylic yarn (3½ oz/180 yds/ 100g per skein):
    - 1 skein each #336 coffee and #353 Donahue
- Size H/8/5mm crochet hook or size needed to obtain gauge
- Tapestry needle

Gauge

14 sts = 4 inches; 8 rows = 4 inches

Pattern Notes

Foundation round and last round are worked with 1 strand of yarn without carrying alternate color.

Weave in ends as work progresses.

Chain-3 at beginning of round counts as first double crochet unless otherwise stated.

Join with slip stitch in the first stitch of each round unless otherwise stated.

When changing color in Pattern Stitch, carry and work over color not in use on wrong side of tapestry crochet section. Do not cut or fasten off unless otherwise stated.

Spiral Pattern can be worked by following written instructions or Chart. Follow Chart rounds 1–11 from right to left.

Pattern Stitch

Spiral Pattern

Rnd 1: With coffee, **ch 3** *(see Pattern Notes)*, working in **back lps** *(see Stitch Guide)*, dc in each of first 24 sc, [**change color** *(see page 5 and Pattern Notes)* to Donahue, dc in each of next 25 sc*, change color to coffee, dc in each of next 25 sc] 4 times ending last rep at *, join. *(200 dc)*

Rnd 2: With coffee, ch 3, working in back lps, dc in next dc, [change color to Donahue, dc in each of next 21 dc, change color to coffee, dc in each of next 2 dc, change color to Donahue, dc in each of next 2 dc, change color to coffee, dc in each of next 21 dc, change color to Donahue, dc in each of next 2 dc, change color to coffee*, dc in each of next 2 dc] 4 times, ending last rep at *, join.

Rnd 3: With coffee, ch 3, working in back lps, dc in each of next 20 dc, [change color to Donahue, dc in each of next 2 dc, change color to coffee, dc in each of next 2 dc, change color to Donahue, dc in each of next 21 dc, change color to coffee, dc in each of next 2 dc, change color to Donahue, dc in each of next 2 dc, change color to coffee*, dc in each of next 21 dc] 4 times, ending last rep at *, join.

Rnd 4: With coffee, ch 3, working in back lps, dc in next dc, *change color to Donahue, dc in each of next 17 dc, [change color to coffee, dc in each of next 2 dc, change color to Donahue, dc in each of next 2 dc] twice, change color to coffee, dc in each of next 17 dc**, [change color to Donahue, dc in each of next 2 dc, change color to coffee, dc in each of next 2 dc] twice, rep from * around, ending last rep at **, change color to Donahue, dc in each of next 2 dc, change color to coffee, dc in each of next 2 dc, change color to Donahue, dc in each of last 2 dc, join.

Rnd 6: With coffee, ch 3, working in back lps, dc in next dc, change color to Donahue, dc in each of next 2 dc, change color to coffee, dc in each of next 2 dc, *change color to Donahue, dc in each of next 9 dc, [change color to coffee, dc in each of next 2 dc, change color to Donahue, dc in each of next 2 dc] 4 times, change color to coffee, dc in each of next 9 dc**, [change color to Donahue, dc in each of next 2 dc, change color to coffee, dc in each of next 2 dc] 4 times, rep from * around, ending last rep at **, [change color to Donahue, dc in each of next 2 dc, change color to coffee, dc in each of next 2 dc] twice, change color to Donahue, dc in each of last 2 dc, join.

Rnd 7: With coffee, ch 3, working in back lps, dc in next dc, change color to Donahue, dc in each of next 2 dc, change color to coffee, dc in each of next 2 dc, change color to Donahue, dc in each of next 2 dc, *change color to coffee, dc in each of next 9 dc, [change color to Donahue, dc in each of next 2 dc, change color to coffee, dc in each of next 2 dc] 4 times, change color to Donahue, dc in each of next 9 dc**, [change color to coffee, dc in each of next 2 dc, change color to Donahue, dc in each of next 2 dc] 4 times, rep from * around, ending last rep at **, [change color to coffee, dc in each of next 2 dc, change color to Donahue, dc in each of next 2 dc] twice, join.

Rnd 5: With coffee, ch 3, working in back lps, dc in next dc, change color to Donahue, dc in each of next 2 dc, *change color to coffee, dc in each of next 13 dc, [change color to Donahue, dc in each of next 2 dc, change color to coffee, dc in each of next 2 dc] 3 times, change color to Donahue, dc in each of next 13 dc**, [change color to coffee, dc in each of next 2 dc, change color to Donahue, dc in each of next 2 dc] 3 times, rep from * around, ending last rep at **, [change color to coffee, dc in each of next 2 dc, change color to Donahue, dc in each of next 2 dc] twice, join.

Rnd 8: With coffee, ch 3, working in back lps, dc in next dc, change color to Donahue, dc in each of next 2 dc, change color to coffee, dc in each of next 2 dc, *change color to Donahue, dc in each of next 13 dc, [change color to coffee, dc in each of next 2 dc, change color to Donahue, dc in each of next 2 dc] 3 times, change color to coffee, dc in each of next 13 dc**, [change color to Donahue, dc in each of next 2 dc, change color to coffee, dc in each of next 2 dc] 3 times, rep from * around, ending last rep at **, change color to Donahue, dc in each of next 2 dc, change color to coffee, dc in each of next 2 dc, change color to Donahue, dc in each of last 2 dc, join.

Rnd 9: With coffee, ch 3, working in back lps, dc in next dc, change color to Donahue, dc in each of next 2 dc, *change color to coffee, dc in each of next 17 dc, [change color to Donahue, dc in each of next 2 dc, change color to coffee, dc in each of next 2 dc] twice, change color to Donahue, dc in each of next 17 dc**, [change color to coffee, dc in each of next 2 dc, change color to Donahue, dc in each of next 2 dc] twice, rep from * around, ending last rep at **, change color to coffee, dc in each of next 2 dc, change color to Donahue, dc in each of last 2 dc, join.

Rnd 10: Rep rnd 2.

Rnd 11: Rep rnd 1. Cut Donahue.

Cowl

Foundation rnd: With coffee, ch 200, **join** *(see Pattern Notes)* in the first ch made, to close in the round. Ch 1, sc in each ch around, join. *(200 sc)*

Rnds 1–11: Work rnds 1–11 of **Spiral Pattern** *(see Pattern Stitch)*.

Last rnd: With coffee, ch 1, working back lps, sc in each dc around, join. Fasten off. ●

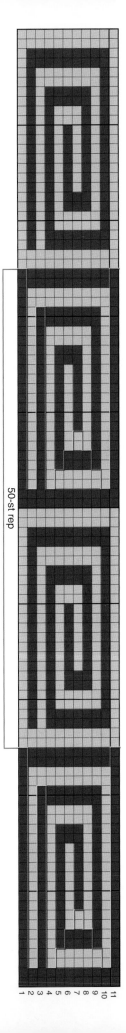

COLOR KEY
■ Coffee
▨ Donahue

Spiraling Cowl
Color Chart

50-st rep

Blending Colors Hat

Skill Level

 INTERMEDIATE

Finished Sizes

Instructions given fit teen; changes for woman and man are in [ ].

Materials

- Universal Yarn Uptown DK light (DK) weight acrylic yarn (3½ oz/273 yds/100g per skein):
    1 skein each #129 iron, #125 silver and #106 bittersweet

3 LIGHT

- Size G/6/4mm crochet hook or size needed to obtain gauge
- Tapestry needle
- Stitch marker

Finished Measurements

Circumference: 19 [21¼, 23] inches

Length: 7 [7½, 8] inches tall

Gauge

20 sts = 4 inches; 17 rows = 4 inches

Pattern Notes

Ribbing, foundation rounds and Crown are worked with 1 strand of yarn without carrying alternate color.

When working the tapestry crochet portion, do not tighten or pull the wrapped yarn as this will make the Hat fit too tightly on the head.

Weave in ends as work progresses.

Join with slip stitch in the first stitch of each round unless otherwise stated.

Chain-3 at beginning of round counts as first double crochet unless otherwise stated.

Place marker on first stitch of round and move up as each round is completed.

When changing color in Pattern Stitch, carry and work over color not in use on wrong side of tapestry crochet section. Do not cut or fasten off unless otherwise stated.

Blending Colors Pattern can be worked by following written instructions or Chart. Follow Chart rows 1–20 from right to left.

Special Stitch
Increase (inc): 2 sc in indicated st.

Pattern Stitch
Blending Colors Pattern

Rnd 1: With iron, ch 1, working in **back lps** *(see Stitch Guide)*, sc in each of first 3 sc, ***change color** (see page 5 and Pattern Notes)* to silver, sc in next sc, change color to iron, sc in each of next 5 sc, rep 14 [16, 18] times from * around, change color to silver, sc in next sc, change color to iron, sc in each of last 2 sc, join. *(96 [108, 120] sc)*

Rnd 2: With iron, ch 1, working in back lps, sc in each sc around, join.

Rnd 3: With iron, ch 1, working in back lps, sc in each of first 2 sc, *change color to silver, sc in next st, change color to iron**, sc in each of next 2 sc, rep 31 [35, 39] times from * around, ending last rep at **, join.

Rnd 4: With iron, ch 1, working in back lps, sc in each sc around, join, change color to silver.

Rnd 5: Ch 1, working in back lps, sc in first sc, *change color to iron**, sc in next sc, change color to silver, sc in next sc, rep 47 [53, 59] times from * around, ending last rep at **, join.

Rnd 6: With iron, ch 1, working in back lps, sc in first sc, *change color to silver, sc in next sc**, change color to iron, sc in next sc, rep 47 [53, 59] times from * around, ending last rep at **, join.

Rnd 7: With silver, ch 1, working in back lps, sc in each of first 2 sc, *change color to iron, sc in next sc, change color to silver**, sc in each of next 2 sc, rep 31 [35, 39] times from * around, ending last rep at **, join.

Rnd 8: With silver, ch 1, working in back lps, sc in each sc around, join.

Rnd 9: With silver, ch 1, working in back lps, sc in each of first 3 sc, *change color to iron, sc in next sc, change color to silver, sc in each of next 5 sc, rep 14 [16, 18] times from * around, change color to iron, sc in next sc, change color to silver, sc in each of last 2 sc, join.

Rnds 10 & 11: Rep rnd 8.

Rnd 12: With silver, ch 1, working in back lps, sc in first sc, *change color to bittersweet, sc in next sc, change color to silver, sc in each of next 5 sc, rep 14 [16, 18] times from * around, change color to bittersweet, sc in next sc, change color to silver, sc in each of last 4 sc, join.

Rnd 13: Rep rnd 8.

Rnd 14: With silver, ch 1, working in back lps, sc in each of first 2 sc, *change color to bittersweet, sc in next st**, change color to silver, sc in each of next 2 sc, rep 31 [35, 39] times from * around, ending last rep at **, join.

Rnd 15: Ch 1, working in back lps, sc in first sc, *change color to silver, sc in next sc**, change color to bittersweet, sc in next sc, rep 47 [53, 59] times from * around, ending last rep at **, join.

Rnd 16: Ch 1, working in back lps, sc in first sc, *change color to bittersweet**, sc in next sc, change color to silver, sc in next sc, rep 47 [53, 59] times from * around, ending last rep at **, join.

Rnd 17: With bittersweet, ch 1, working in back lps, sc in each sc around, join.

Rnd 18: With bittersweet, ch 1, working in back lps, sc in each of first 2 sc, *change color to silver, sc in next st, change color to bittersweet**, sc in each of next 2 sc, rep 31 [35, 39] times from * around, ending last rep at **, join.

Rnd 19: Rep rnd 17.

Rnd 20: With bittersweet, ch 1, working in back lps, sc in each of first 3 sc, *change color to silver, sc in next sc, change color to bittersweet, sc in each of next 5 sc, rep 14 [16, 18] times from * around, change color to silver, sc in next sc, change color to bittersweet, sc in each of last 2 sc, join.

Hat

Ribbing

Rnd 1: With iron, ch 84 [96, 108] loosely, **join** *(see Pattern Notes)* in first ch made to close the rnd. **Ch 3** *(see Pattern Notes)*, dc in each ch around, join. **Place marker** *(see Pattern Notes)* on first st. *(84 [96, 108] dc)*

Rnd 2: With iron, ch 3, **fpdc** *(see Stitch Guide)* in next dc**, **bpdc** *(see Stitch Guide)* in next dc, rep 41 [47, 53] times from * around, ending last rep at **, join. *(84 [96, 108] dc)*

Body

Foundation rnd 1: With iron, ch 1, working in back lps, sc in each of first 6 [7, 8] dc, **inc** *(see Special Stitch)* in next dc, *sc in each of next 6 [7, 8] dc, inc in next dc, rep 10 times from * around, join. *(96 [108, 120] sc)*

Foundation rnd 2: With iron, ch 1, working in back lps, sc in each sc around, join.

Rnds 1–20: Work rnds 1–20 of **Blending Colors Pattern** *(see Pattern Stitch)*. Cut silver.

Sizes Woman & Man Only

Next rnd: With bittersweet, ch 1, working in back lps, sc in each sc around, join. *(108 [120] sc)*

Size Man Only

Next rnd: With bittersweet, ch 1, working in back lps, sc in each sc around, join. *(120 sc)*

Crown

All Sizes

Next rnd: With bittersweet, ch 1, working in back lps, sc in each of first 6 [7, 8] sc, **sc dec** *(see Stitch Guide)* in next 2 sc, *sc in each of next 6 [7, 8] sc, sc dec in next 2 sc, rep 10 times from * around, join. *(84 [96, 108] sc)*

Next rnd: With bittersweet, ch 1, working in back lps, sc in each of first 5 [6, 7] sc, sc dec in next 2 sc, *sc in each of next 5 [6, 7] sc, sc dec in next 2 sc, rep 10 times from * around, join. *(72 [84, 96] sc)*

Next rnd: With bittersweet, ch 1, working in back lps, sc in each of first 4 [5, 6] sc, sc dec in next 2 sc, *sc in each of next 4 [5, 6] sc, sc dec in next 2 sc, rep 10 times from * around, join. *(60 [72, 84] sc)*

Next rnd: With bittersweet, ch 1, working in back lps, sc in each of first 3 [4, 5] sc, sc dec in next 2 sc, *sc in each of next 3 [4, 5] sc, sc dec in next 2 sc, rep 10 times from * around, join. *(48 [60, 72] sc)*

Next rnd: With bittersweet, ch 1, working in back lps, sc in each of first 2 [3, 4] sc, sc dec in next 2 sc, *sc in each of next 2 [3, 4] sc, sc dec in next 2 sc, rep 10 times from * around, join. *(36 [48, 60] sc)*

Next rnd: With bittersweet, ch 1, working in back lps, sc in each of first 1 [2, 3] sc, sc dec in next 2 sc, *sc in each of next 1 [2, 3] sc, sc dec in next 2 sc, rep 10 times from * around, join. *(24 [36, 48] sc)*

Size Teen Only

Last rnd: With bittersweet, ch 1, working in back lps, sc dec in first 2 sc, [sc dec in next 2 sc] 11 times, join. Leaving an 8-inch tail, fasten off. *(12 sc)*

Sizes Woman & Man Only

Next rnd: With bittersweet, ch 1, working in back lps, sc in each of first 1 [2] sc, sc dec in next 2 sc, *sc in each of next 1 [2] sc, sc dec in next 2 sc, rep 10 times from * around, join. *(24 [36] sc)*

Size Woman Only

Last rnd: With bittersweet, ch 1, working in back lps, sc dec in first 2 sc, [sc dec in next 2 sc] 11 times, join. Leaving an 8-inch tail, fasten off. *(12 sc)*

Size Man Only

Next rnd: With bittersweet, ch 1, working in back lps, sc in first sc, sc dec in next 2 sc, *sc in next sc, sc dec in next 2 sc, rep 10 times from * around, join. *(24 sc)*

Last rnd: With bittersweet, ch 1, working in back lps, sc dec in first 2 sc, [sc dec in next 2 sc] 11 times, join. Leaving an 8-inch tail, fasten off. *(12 sc)*

Finishing

Weave tail through last rnd and pull tightly to close Crown. Secure tail. ●

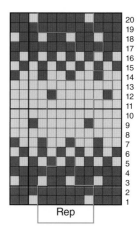

Blending Colors Hat
Color Chart

COLOR KEY
■ Iron
□ Silver
■ Bittersweet

Spanish
Tile Bag

Skill Level

Finished Measurements

14 inches wide x 11 inches long, excluding Handles

Materials

- Omega Sinfonia light (DK) weight mercerized cotton yarn (3½ oz/218 yds/100g per skein):
    2 skeins each #802 cream and
    #813 denim
    1 skein #843 dark cinnamon
- Sizes E/4/3.5mm and H/8/5mm crochet hooks or size needed to obtain gauge
- Tapestry needle
- Stitch marker

3 LIGHT

Gauge

With E hook: 22 sts = 4 inches; 6 rnds = 2¾ inches

Pattern Notes

For durability and strength, carry and wrap alternate colors not in use in all rounds from foundation round 2 of Bottom through end of Body.

Handles, Drawstring and Stopper are worked with 1 strand of yarn.

Weave in ends as work progresses.

Join with slip stitch in the first stitch of each round unless otherwise stated.

Place marker on first stitch of round and move up as each round is completed.

When changing color in Pattern Stitch, carry and work over colors not in use on wrong side of tapestry crochet section. Do not cut or fasten off unless otherwise stated.

Spanish Tile Pattern can be worked by following written instructions or Chart. Follow Chart rounds 1–14 from right to left.

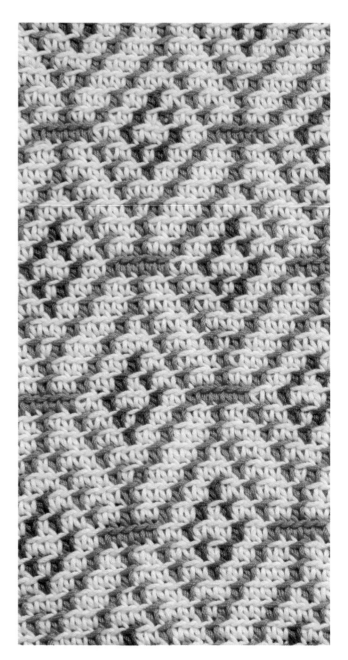

Special Stitch

Increase (inc): 2 sc in indicated st.

Pattern Stitch
Spanish Tile Pattern

Rnd 1: With cinnamon, ch 1, working in back lps), sc in each of first 3 sc, [**change color** *(see page 5 and Pattern Notes)* to cream, sc in each of next 2 sc, change color to denim, sc in next sc, change color to cream, sc in each of next 3 sc, change color to denim, sc in next sc, change color to cream, sc in each of next 2 sc, change color to cinnamon*, sc in each of next 5 sc] 11 times, ending last rep at *, sc in each of last 2 sc, join. *(168 sc)*

Rnd 2: With cinnamon, ch 1, working in back lps, sc in first sc, change color to cream, sc in each of next 2 sc, change color to cinnamon, sc in next sc, change color to cream, sc in each of next 2 sc, *change color to denim, sc in next sc, change color to cream, sc in next sc, change color to denim, sc in next sc**, [change color to cream, sc in each of next 2 sc, change color to cinnamon, sc in next sc] 3 times, change color to cream, sc in each of next 2 sc, rep 11 times from * around, ending last rep at **, change color to cream, sc in each of next 2 sc, change color to cinnamon, sc in next sc, change color to cream, sc in each of last 2 sc, join.

Rnd 3: With cinnamon, ch 1, working in back lps, sc in first sc, change color to cream, sc in each of next 3 sc, *change color to cinnamon, sc in next sc, change color to cream, sc in each of next 2 sc, change color to denim, sc in next sc, change color to cream, sc in each of next 2 sc**, [change color to cinnamon, sc in next sc, change color to cream, sc in each of next 3 sc] twice, rep 11 times from * around, ending last rep at **, change color to cinnamon, sc in next sc, change color to cream, sc in each of last 3 sc, join.

Rnd 4: With cream, ch 1, working in back lps, sc in first sc, *[change color to cinnamon, sc in next sc, change color to cream, sc in each of next 3 sc] 3 times, change color to cinnamon, sc in next sc, change color to cream**, sc in next sc, rep 11 times from * around, ending last rep at **, join.

Rnd 5: Ch 1, sc each of first 2 sc, change color to cinnamon, sc in next sc, change color to cream, sc in each of next 3 sc, *change color to cinnamon, sc in next sc, change color to cream, sc in next sc**, [change color to cinnamon, sc in next sc, change color to cream, sc in each of next 3 sc] 3 times, rep 11 times from * around, ending last rep at **, change color to cinnamon, sc in next sc, change color to cream, sc in each of next 3 sc, change color to cinnamon, sc in next sc, change color to cream, sc in last sc, join, change color to denim.

Rnd 6: Ch 1, working in back lps, sc in first sc, *change color to cream, sc in each of next 2 sc, [change color to cinnamon, sc in next sc, change color to cream, sc in each of next 3 sc] twice, change color to cinnamon, sc in next sc, change color to cream, sc in each of next 2 sc**, change color to denim, sc in next sc, rep 11 times from * around, ending last rep at **, join.

Rnd 7: With cream, ch 1, working in back lps, sc in first sc, *change color to denim, sc in next sc, [change color to cream, sc in each of next 2 sc, change color to cinnamon, sc in next sc] 3 times, change color to cream, sc in each of next 2 sc, change color to denim, sc in next sc**, change color to cream, sc in next sc, rep 11 times from * around, ending last rep at **, join.

Rnd 8: With cream, ch 1, sc in each of next 2 sc, *change color to denim, sc in next sc, change color to cream, sc in each of next 2 sc, change color to cinnamon, sc in each of next 5 sc, change color to cream, sc in each of next 2 sc, change color to denim, sc in next sc, change color to cream**, sc in each of next 3 sc, rep 11 times from * around, ending last rep at **, sc in last sc, join.

Rnd 9: Rep rnd 7.

Rnd 10: Rep rnd 6.

Rnd 11: Rep rnd 5.

Rnd 12: Rep rnd 4.

Rnd 13: Rep rnd 3.

Rnd 14: Rep rnd 2.

Bag

Bottom

With cream and size E hook, make a **slip ring** (see illustration).

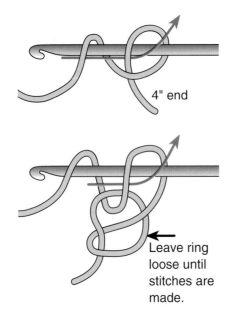

4" end

← Leave ring loose until stitches are made.

Slip Ring

Foundation rnd 1: Ch 1, 5 sc in ring, **join** (see Pattern Notes) in beg sc. (5 sc)

Foundation rnd 2: With cream, ch 1, working in **back lps** (see Stitch Guide), **inc** (see Special Stitch) in each of next 5 sc, join. (10 sc)

Foundation rnd 3: With cream, ch 1, working in back lps, inc in each of next 10 sc, join. (20 sc)

Foundation rnd 4: With cream, ch 1, working in back lps, [sc in next sc, inc in next sc] 10 times, join. (30 sc)

Foundation rnd 5: With cream, ch 1, working in back lps, [sc in each of next 2 sc, inc in next sc] 10 times, join. (40 sc)

Foundation rnd 6: With cream, ch 1, working in back lps, [sc in each of next 3 sc, inc in next sc] 10 times, change color to denim, join. (50 sc)

Foundation rnd 7: With denim, ch 1, working in back lps, [sc in each of next 4 sc, inc in next sc] 10 times, join. (60 sc)

Foundation rnd 8: With denim, ch 1, working in back lps, [sc in each of next 5 sc, inc in next sc] 10 times, join. (70 sc)

Foundation rnd 9: With denim, ch 1, working in back lps, [sc in each of next 6 sc, inc in next sc] 10 times, join. (80 sc)

Foundation rnd 10: With denim, ch 1, working in back lps, [sc in each of next 7 sc, inc in next sc] 10 times, join. (90 sc)

Foundation rnd 11: With denim, ch 1, working in back lps, [sc in each of next 8 sc, inc in next sc] 10 times, join. (100 sc)

Foundation rnd 12: With denim, ch 1, working in back lps, [sc in each of next 9 sc, inc in next sc] 10 times, change color to cinnamon, join. (110 sc)

Foundation rnd 13: With cinnamon, ch 1, working in back lps, [sc in each of next 10 sc, inc in next sc] 10 times, join. (120 sc)

Foundation rnd 14: With cinnamon, ch 1, working in back lps, [sc in each of next 11 sc, inc in next sc] 10 times, join. (130 sc)

Foundation rnd 15: With cinnamon, ch 1, working in back lps, [sc in each of next 12 sc, inc in next sc] 10 times, join. (140 sc)

Foundation rnd 16: With cinnamon, ch 1, working in back lps, [sc in each of next 13 sc, inc in next sc] 10 times, join. (150 sc)

Foundation rnd 17: With cinnamon, ch 1, working in back lps, [sc in each of next 14 sc, inc in next sc] 10 times, join. (160 sc)

Foundation rnd 18: With cinnamon, ch 1, working in back lps, [sc in each of next 19 sc, inc in next sc] 8 times, join. (168 sc)

Body

Rnds 1–36: Work rnds 1–14 of **Spanish Tile Pattern** *(see Pattern Stitch)* twice and then rnds 1–8 once more.

Continue working over cream and cinnamon held tog.

Next 2 rnds: With denim, ch 1, working in back lps, sc in each sc across, join. *(168 sc)*

Next rnd: With denim, ch 1, working in back lps, sc in each of next 8 sc, [working over cream and cinnamon, work 5 sc *(see photos 37 and 38 on page 9—eyelet made)*, sk 5 sc, sc in each of next 16 sc] 7 times, working over cream and cinnamon, work 5 sc *(eyelet made)*, sk 5 sc, sc in each of next 8 sc, join. *(168 sc, 8 eyelets)*

Next 3 rnds: With denim, ch 1, working in back lps, sc in each sc across, join. Fasten off.

Handles
Make 2.

Leaving a long tail for sewing, with 2 strands of denim held tog and H hook, ch 77.

Rnd 1: Make 2 sc in 2nd ch from hook, sc in each of next 74 chs, 3 sc in next ch, continue on other side of the foundation ch, sk first ch, sc in each of last 75 chs, join. *(154 sc)*

Rnd 2: Ch 1, 3 sc in first sc, sc in each of next 76 sc, 3 sc in next sc, sc in each of last 76 sc, join. Fasten off leaving a long tail for sewing. *(158 sc)*

Drawstring

With 2 strands of denim held tog and H hook, ch 157.

Row 1: Starting in 2nd ch from the hook, sl st in each of next 156 chs. *(156 sl sts)*

Fasten off.

Stopper

With denim and E hook, ch 10. Join in first ch made to close the round.

Rnd 1: Ch 1, sc in each of next 10 chs. Do not join here or throughout unless stated otherwise. *(10 sc)*

Continue working in a spiral way.

Rnds 2–5: Sc in each of next 10 sc. At end of last rnd, join. Fasten off, leaving a long tail for sewing.

Assembly

Sew each Handle to front and back of the Bag, placing each end between 2 eyelets.

Pull the Drawstring through the eyelets, starting in 1 of 2 center eyelets (front to back) until it comes out on the same side from the other center eyelet.

With the long tail of the Stopper make a seam in the middle from top to bottom, to divide it in 2 sections. Pull each end of the Drawstring through the stopper; it should feel a bit tight.

Make a knot on each end of the Drawstring. ●

COLOR KEY
- ■ Dark cinnamon
- ■ Denim
- □ Cream

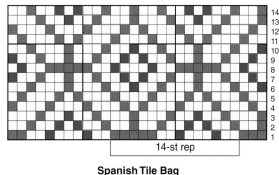

14-st rep

Spanish Tile Bag
Color Chart

Peaked Waves Slippers

Skill Level

 INTERMEDIATE

Finished Sizes

Instructions given fit size small; changes for medium and large are in [ ].

Materials

- Berroco Vintage medium (worsted) weight acrylic/wool/nylon yarn (3½ oz/218 yds/100g per hank):
  1 hank each #5181 black cherry, #5175 fennel and #5122 banane
- Size 7/4.5mm crochet hook or size needed to obtain gauge
- Tapestry needle
- Stitch marker

4

MEDIUM

Finished Measurements

Foot length: 8 [9, 10¼] inches, measured across sole

Width: 3⅜ [4⁵⁄₁₆, 5⁵⁄₁₆] inches, measured flat

Gauge

21 sts = 4 inches; 16 rows = 4 inches

Pattern Notes

Slipper is worked from the Toe to the Heel, then finished at the ankle.

All sections except Foot Cover are worked with 1 strand of yarn without carrying alternate color.

When working the tapestry crochet portion, do not tighten or pull the wrapped yarn as this could make the Slippers fit tightly around the foot.

Weave in ends as work progresses.

Join with slip stitch in the first stitch of each round unless otherwise stated.

Place marker on first stitch of round and move up as each round is completed.

When changing color in Pattern Stitch, carry and work over color not in use on wrong side of tapestry crochet section. Do not cut or fasten off unless otherwise stated.

Peaked Waves Pattern can be worked by following written instructions or Chart. Follow Chart rows 1–12 from right to left.

Special Stitch

Increase (inc): 2 sc in indicated st.

Pattern Stitch

Peaked Waves Pattern

Rnd 1: With banane, ch 1, working in **back lps** (see Stitch Guide), sc in each of first 4 sc, *change color (see page 5 and Pattern Notes) to black cherry, sc in next sc, change color to banane**, sc in each of next 4 sc, rep 5 [7, 9] times from * around, ending last rep at **, join. (35 [45, 55] sc)

Rnd 2: With banane, ch 1, working in back lps, sc in each of first 3 sc, *change color to black cherry, sc in each of next 2 sc, change color to banane**, sc in each of next 3 sc, rep 5 [7, 9] times from * around, ending last rep at **, join.

Rnd 3: With banane, working in back lps, ch 1, sc in each of first 2 sc, *change color to black cherry, sc in each of next 3 sc, change color to banane**, work in next 2 sc, rep 5 [7, 9] times from * around, ending last rep at **, join.

Rnd 4: With banane, working in back lps, ch 1, sc in first sc, *change color to black cherry, sc in each of next 2 sc, change color to banane, sc in next sc, change color to black cherry, sc in next sc**, change color to banane, sc in next sc, rep 6 [8, 8] times from * around, ending last rep at **, join.

Rnd 5: With black cherry, working in back lps, ch 1, sc in each of first 2 sc, *change color to banane, sc in each of next 2 sc, change color to black cherry**, sc in each of next 3 sc, rep 6 [8, 10] times from * around, ending last rep at **, sc in last sc, join.

Rnd 6: With black cherry, working in back lps, ch 1, sc in first sc, *change color to banane, sc in each of next 3 sc, change color to black cherry**, sc in each of next 2 sc, rep 6 [8, 10] times from * around, ending last rep at **, sc in last sc, change color to fennel, join. Cut black cherry.

Rnd 7: With fennel, working in back lps, ch 1, sc in each of first 4 sc, *change color to banane, sc in next sc, change color to fennel**, sc in each of next 4 sc, rep 6 [8, 10] times from * around, ending last rep at **, join.

Rnd 8: With fennel, working in back lps, ch 1, sc in each of first 3 sc, *change color to banane, sc in each of next 2 sc, change color to fennel**, sc in each of next 3 sc, rep 6 [8, 10] times from * around, ending last rep at **, join.

Rnd 9: With fennel, working in back lps, ch 1, sc in each of next 2 sc, *change color to banane, sc in each of next 3 sc, change color to fennel**, sc in each of next 2 sc, rep 6 [8, 10] times from * around, ending last rep at **, join.

Rnd 10: With fennel, working in back lps, ch 1, sc in first sc, *change color to banane, sc in each of next 2 sc, change color to fennel, sc in next sc, change color to banane, sc in next sc**, change color to fennel, sc in next sc, rep 6 [8, 8] times from * around, ending last rep at **, join.

Rnd 11: With banane, working in back lps, ch 1, sc in each of first 2 sc, *change color to fennel, sc in each of next 2 sc, change color to banane**, sc in each of next 3 sc, rep 6 [8, 10] times from * around, ending last rep at **, sc in last sc, join.

Rnd 12: With banane, working in back lps, ch 1, sc in first sc, *change color to fennel, sc in each of next 3 sc, change color to banane**, sc in each of next 2 sc, rep 6 [8, 10] times from * around, ending last rep at **, sc in last sc, change color to black cherry, join. Cut fennel and banane.

Slippers

Toe

All Sizes
Foundation rnd 1: With fennel, ch 10 [15, 20], working in back lps, **inc** (see Special Stitch) in 2nd ch from the hook, sc in each of next 7 [12, 17] chs, 4 sc in next ch, continue on the other side of the foundation ch, sk first ch, sc in each of next 7 [12, 17] chs, inc in last ch, **join** (see Pattern Notes). (22 [32, 42] sc)

Foundation rnd 2: With fennel, working in back lps, ch 1, inc in first sc, sc in each of next 9 [14, 19] sc, [inc in next sc] twice, sc in each of next 9 [14, 19] sc, inc in last sc, join. (26 [36, 46] sc)

Foundation rnd 3: With fennel, working in back lps, ch 1, inc in first sc, sc in each of next 11 [16, 21] sc, [inc in next sc] twice, sc in each of next 11 [16, 21] sc, inc in last sc, join. (30 [40, 50] sc)

Foundation rnd 4: With fennel, working in back lps, ch 1, inc in first sc, sc in each of next 13 [18, 23] sc, [inc in next sc] twice, sc in each of next 13 [18, 23] sc, inc in last sc, join. (34 [44, 54] sc)

Foundation rnd 5: With fennel, working in back lps, ch 1, sc in each of first 25 [33, 41] sc, inc in next sc, sc in each of last 8 [10, 12] sc, join. (35 [45, 55] sc)

Foot Cover

Size Small Only
Rnds 1–12: Work rnds 1–12 of **Peaked Waves Pattern** (see Pattern Stitch).

Size Medium Only

Foundation rnds 6 & 7: With fennel, working in back lps, ch 1, sc in each sc around, join. *(45 sc)*

Rnds 1–12: Work rnds 1–12 of **Peaked Waves Pattern** *(see Pattern Stitch).*

Size Large Only

Foundation rnds 6–11: With fennel, working in back lps, ch 1, sc in each sc around, join. *(55 sc)*

Rnds 1–12: Work rnds 1–12 of **Peaked Waves Pattern** *(see Pattern Stitch).*

All Sizes

Next rnd: With black cherry, ch 1, sc in each sc around, join. *(35 [45, 55] sc)* Fasten off.

Heel

With RS of Toe facing, counting from right to left from the join, attach black cherry to 13th [17th, 20th] st. Continue working in turned rows.

Size Small Only

Rows 1–18: Ch 1, sc in each of first 28 sts, leave rem sts unworked, turn. *(28 sc)*

Size Medium Only

Rows 1–20: Ch 1, sc in each of first 36 sts, leave rem sts unworked, turn. *(36 sc)*

Size Large Only

Rows 1–22: Ch 1, sc in each of first 44 sts, leave rem sts unworked, turn. *(44 sc)*

All Sizes

Next row: With black cherry, ch 1, sc in each of first 12 [16, 20] sc, [**sc dec** *(see Stitch Guide)* in next 2 sc] twice, sc in each of next 12 [16, 20] sc, turn. *(26 [34, 42] sc)*

Next row: With black cherry, ch 1, sc in each of next 11 [15, 19] sc, [sc dec in next 2 sc] twice, sc in each of next 11 [15, 19] sc, turn. *(24 [32, 40] sc)*

Next row: With black cherry, ch 1, sc in each of next 10 [14, 18] sc, [sc dec in next 2 sc] twice, sc in each of next 10 [14, 18] sc, turn. *(22 [30, 38] sc)*

Leaving a long tail for sewing, fasten off.

Hold edges of last row tog and sew the back of Heel. With RS facing, join black cherry at back of Heel. Continue crocheting in rnds for Ankle.

Ankle

All Sizes

Next rnd: With black cherry, ch 1, sc in ends of each of first 21 [23, 25] rows, sc in each of next 7 [9, 11] sc, sc in ends of each of last 21 [23, 25] rows, join. *(49 [55, 61] sc)*

Size Small Only

Next rnd: With black cherry, working in back lps, ch 1, sc in first sc, [sc dec in next 2 sc, sc in each of next 2 sc, sc dec in next 2 sc*, sc in next sc] 7 times, ending last rep at *, change color to banane, join. *(35 sc)*

Next 8 rnds: With banane, ch 1, working in back lps, sc in each sc around, join. Fasten off.

Size Medium Only

Next rnd: With black cherry, ch 1, working in back lps, sc in each of first 3 sc, [sc dec in next 2 sc, sc in each of next 4 sc, sc dec in next 2 sc*, sc in each of next 3 sc] 5 times, ending last rep at *, change color to banane, join. *(45 sc)*

Next 10 rnds: With banane, ch 1, working in back lps, sc in each sc around, join. Fasten off.

Size Large Only

Next rnd: With black cherry, ch 1, working in back lps, sc in each of first 8 sc, [sc dec in next 2 sc*, sc in each of next 8 sc] 5 times, ending last rep at *, sc in each of next 9 sc, sc dec in last 2 sc, change color to banane, join. *(55 sc)*

Next 12 rnds: With banane, ch 1, working in back lps, sc in each sc around, join. Fasten off.

Finishing
Fold Ankle outward. ●

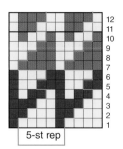

Peaked Waves Slippers
Color Chart

COLOR KEY
☐ Banane
■ Black cherry
▨ Fennel

STITCH GUIDE

STITCH ABBREVIATIONS

beg	begin/begins/beginning
bpdc	back post double crochet
bpsc	back post single crochet
bptr	back post treble crochet
CC	contrasting color
ch(s)	chain(s)
ch-	refers to chain or space previously made (i.e., ch-1 space)
ch sp(s)	chain space(s)
cl(s)	cluster(s)
cm	centimeter(s)
dc	double crochet (singular/plural)
dc dec	double crochet 2 or more stitches together, as indicated
dec	decrease/decreases/decreasing
dtr	double treble crochet
ext	extended
fpdc	front post double crochet
fpsc	front post single crochet
fptr	front post treble crochet
g	gram(s)
hdc	half double crochet
hdc dec	half double crochet 2 or more stitches together, as indicated
inc	increase/increases/increasing
lp(s)	loop(s)
MC	main color
mm	millimeter(s)
oz	ounce(s)
pc	popcorn(s)
rem	remain/remains/remaining
rep(s)	repeat(s)
rnd(s)	round(s)
RS	right side
sc	single crochet (singular/plural)
sc dec	single crochet 2 or more stitches together, as indicated
sk	skip/skipped/skipping
sl st(s)	slip stitch(es)
sp(s)	space(s)/spaced
st(s)	stitch(es)
tog	together
tr	treble crochet
trtr	triple treble
WS	wrong side
yd(s)	yard(s)
yo	yarn over

YARN CONVERSION

OUNCES TO GRAMS	GRAMS TO OUNCES
1 .... 28.4	25 .... ⅞
2 .... 56.7	40 .... 1⅔
3 .... 85.0	50 .... 1¾
4 .... 113.4	100 .... 3½

UNITED STATES		UNITED KINGDOM
sl st (slip stitch)	=	sc (single crochet)
sc (single crochet)	=	dc (double crochet)
hdc (half double crochet)	=	htr (half treble crochet)
dc (double crochet)	=	tr (treble crochet)
tr (treble crochet)	=	dtr (double treble crochet)
dtr (double treble crochet)	=	ttr (triple treble crochet)
skip	=	miss

Single crochet decrease (sc dec): (Insert hook, yo, draw lp through) in each of the sts indicated, yo, draw through all lps on hook.

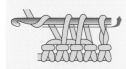

Example of 2-sc dec

Half double crochet decrease (hdc dec): (Yo, insert hook, yo, draw lp through) in each of the sts indicated, yo, draw through all lps on hook.

Example of 2-hdc dec

Reverse single crochet (reverse sc): Ch 1, sk first st, working from left to right, insert hook in next st from front to back, draw up lp on hook, yo and draw through both lps on hook.

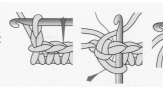

Chain (ch): Yo, pull through lp on hook.

Single crochet (sc): Insert hook in st, yo, pull through st, yo, pull through both lps on hook.

Double crochet (dc): Yo, insert hook in st, yo, pull through st, [yo, pull through 2 lps] twice.

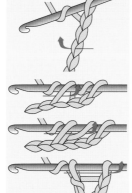

Double crochet decrease (dc dec): (Yo, insert hook, yo, draw lp through, yo, draw through 2 lps on hook) in each of the sts indicated, yo, draw through all lps on hook.

Example of 2-dc dec

Front loop (front lp) Back loop (back lp)

Front Loop   Back Loop

Front post stitch (fp): Back post stitch (bp): When working post st, insert hook from right to left around post of st on previous row.

Back   Front

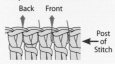

Post of Stitch

Half double crochet (hdc): Yo, insert hook in st, yo, pull through st, yo, pull through all 3 lps on hook.

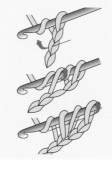

Double treble crochet (dtr): Yo 3 times, insert hook in st, yo, pull through st, [yo, pull through 2 lps] 4 times.

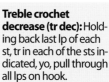

Treble crochet decrease (tr dec): Holding back last lp of each st, tr in each of the sts indicated, yo, pull through all lps on hook.

Example of 2-tr dec

Slip stitch (sl st): Insert hook in st, pull through both lps on hook.

Chain color change (ch color change) Yo with new color, draw through last lp on hook.

Double crochet color change (dc color change) Drop first color, yo with new color, draw through last 2 lps of st.

Treble crochet (tr): Yo twice, insert hook in st, yo, pull through st, [yo, pull through 2 lps] 3 times.

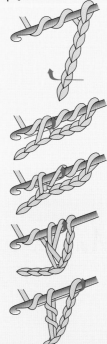

Metric Conversion Charts

METRIC CONVERSIONS

yards	x	.9144	=	metres (m)
yards	x	91.44	=	centimetres (cm)
inches	x	2.54	=	centimetres (cm)
inches	x	25.40	=	millimetres (mm)
inches	x	.0254	=	metres (m)

centimetres	x	.3937	=	inches
metres	x	1.0936	=	yards

INCHES INTO MILLIMETRES & CENTIMETRES (Rounded off slightly)

inches	mm	cm	inches	cm	inches	cm	inches	cm
1/8	3	0.3	5	12.5	21	53.5	38	96.5
1/4	6	0.6	5 1/2	14	22	56	39	99
3/8	10	1	6	15	23	58.5	40	101.5
1/2	13	1.3	7	18	24	61	41	104
5/8	15	1.5	8	20.5	25	63.5	42	106.5
3/4	20	2	9	23	26	66	43	109
7/8	22	2.2	10	25.5	27	68.5	44	112
1	25	2.5	11	28	28	71	45	114.5
1 1/4	32	3.2	12	30.5	29	73.5	46	117
1 1/2	38	3.8	13	33	30	76	47	119.5
1 3/4	45	4.5	14	35.5	31	79	48	122
2	50	5	15	38	32	81.5	49	124.5
2 1/2	65	6.5	16	40.5	33	84	50	127
3	75	7.5	17	43	34	86.5		
3 1/2	90	9	18	46	35	89		
4	100	10	19	48.5	36	91.5		
4 1/2	115	11.5	20	51	37	94		

KNITTING NEEDLES CONVERSION CHART

Canada/U.S.	0	1	2	3	4	5	6	7	8	9	10	10½	11	13	15
Metric (mm)	2	2¼	2¾	3¼	3½	3¾	4	4½	5	5½	6	6½	8	9	10

CROCHET HOOKS CONVERSION CHART

Canada/U.S.	1/B	2/C	3/D	4/E	5/F	6/G	8/H	9/I	10/J	10½/K	N
Metric (mm)	2.25	2.75	3.25	3.5	3.75	4.25	5	5.5	6	6.5	9.0

Annie's® *Learn to Tapestry Crochet* is published by Annie's, 306 East Parr Road, Berne, IN 46711. Printed in USA. Copyright © 2017 Annie's. All rights reserved. This publication may not be reproduced in part or in whole without written permission from the publisher.

RETAIL STORES: If you would like to carry this publication or any other Annie's publication, visit AnniesWSL.com.

Every effort has been made to ensure that the instructions in this publication are complete and accurate. We cannot, however, take responsibility for human error, typographical mistakes or variations in individual work. Please visit AnniesCustomerService.com to check for pattern updates.

ISBN: 978-1-59012-875-6

1 2 3 4 5 6 7 8 9